DATE DUE

DEC 27 1983	JAN 09 2002	
MAY - 4 1984	JAN 06 2004	
FEB 12 1987	JAN 10 2009	
DEC 2 6 1986		
DEC 12 1988	AUG 27 2012	
APR 27 1989		
DEC 16 1991		
DEC 30 1992		
DEC 08 1993	JUL 07 2014	
DEC 8 1994		
DEC 29 1994		
DEC 20 1995		
DEC 24 1996		
DEC 13 1997		

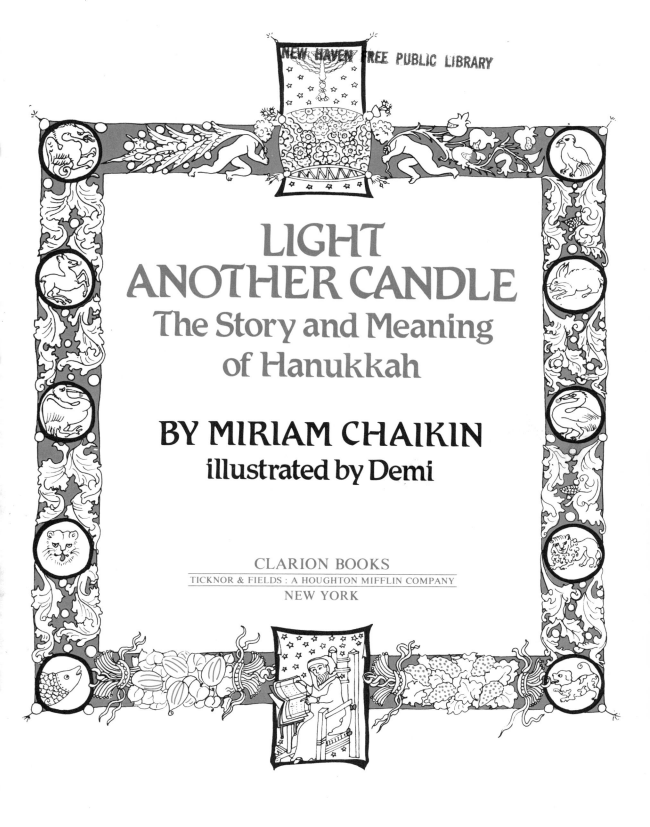

LIGHT ANOTHER CANDLE
The Story and Meaning of Hanukkah

BY MIRIAM CHAIKIN
illustrated by Demi

CLARION BOOKS
TICKNOR & FIELDS : A HOUGHTON MIFFLIN COMPANY
NEW YORK

FOR PAYOO CHAIKIN PEARL AND JACK PEARL

ACKNOWLEDGMENT

I am glad to thank Professor Louis H. Feldman for his careful
reading of the book in manuscript form.

Clarion Books
Ticknor & Fields, a Houghton Mifflin Company
Text copyright © 1981 by Miriam Chaikin
Illustrations copyright © 1981 by Demi
Printed in the United States of America

Library of Congress Cataloging in Publication Data

Chaikin, Miriam.   Light another candle.
Summary: Retells the story of Hanukkah and explains its symbols by
describing high points in Jewish history, worship, and culture.
1. Hanukkah (Feast of Lights)—Juvenile literature. [1. Hanukkah
(Feast of Lights)] I. Title
BM695.H3C45   296.4'35   80-28137   ISBN 0-395-31026-1
Paperback ISBN 0-89919-057-X

CONTENTS

Many Jewish holidays are celebrated in the synagogue, the Jewish house of worship, with song and prayer. But there are very few special prayers for Hanukkah. This two-thousand-year-old Jewish holiday is celebrated primarily in the home.

The hanukkiah, the nine-branch candleholder that is the symbol of this holiday, is removed from the shelf where it has been stored and put in a prominent place. Candles or oil are prepared for burning. And at nightfall, family and friends gather in the living room for the candlelighting ceremony. Then they celebrate the holiday with "mirth and gladness," as Judah the Maccabee commanded their ancestors to do in the year 165 B.C.E.

The story of Judah and the Maccabees does not appear in the Hebrew bible, which Gentiles call the Old Testament, to distinguish it from the New Testament. The Hebrew Bible, according to some scholars, was put together over a period of some four hundred years, from about 300 B.C.E. to 100 C.E. The ancient Jewish sages who compiled the Bible included in it only what they regarded as sacred writings.

There are two major written accounts of the Maccabean period, but neither met the standards of sacredness set up by the sages. One version differed from the other, and the people who wrote them were unknown. Hence the scholars excluded them from the Hebrew Bible.

The two accounts appear in a separate book called Apocrypha, as I Maccabees and II Maccabees. *Apocrypha* means "hidden." It is not certain what this refers to—the hidden or unknown identity of the authors, the fact that the works remained hidden, or undiscovered, for hundreds of years, or both.

Light Another Candle tells the story of the Maccabees and explores the meaning of the issues for which the Jews fought then and which still have great significance for Jews today. It answers such questions as "What does B.C.E. mean?," "What was the Temple?," "What is meant by Jewish law?" and "How is Hanukkah celebrated?"

«THERE IS
BUT ONE GOD»

More than two thousand years ago Alexander the Great conquered all the lands between Greece and India. In the center of these lands was Judea. This was the ancient name for Israel.

Judea was surrounded by rich and cultivated lands. To the north were Babylon and Syria. Egypt lay to the south. To reach one country or the other, the armies of ambitious conquerors and kings had to pass through Judea. It was a corridor between north and south. As such it was often a battleground.

The Jews of Judea had become accustomed to foreign rulers. Before Alexander, the Persians ruled Judea. Before the Persians, the Babylonians governed the land. The Jews of Judea did not care who made the laws so long as they were free to live as Jews. Under Alexander, they were. He ruled from Greece and appointed ministers to govern each land. Not only did he grant the Jews religious freedom, but he protected it.

Writing to his officers in Jerusalem, the capital of Judea, Alexander said:

Judea was one of the lands Alexander conquered.

Alexander, conqueror and king, to his appointed governors in Judea. Greeting. The Jews pay their taxes and keep our laws. Repay them with good. Let no one interfere with their right to live as Jews.

To the Jews, Alexander wrote separately, saying:

Alexander, conqueror and king, to his friends, the Jews. Greeting. Because you are good citizens and offer us friendship, we will protect you. May all go well with your nation, and may sword and enemy be far from you.

The Jews answered:

The Jews of Judea to Alexander, conqueror and king. Peace. The Jewish nation thanks you for your protection and prays for your health.

While the Jews obeyed Alexander's law, they also obeyed the Jewish law. They did not eat the flesh of a pig. They circumcised infant boys. They kept the Sabbath. On each Sabbath and festival day they went to the Temple in Jerusalem to pray.

But peace was soon over for the Jews. When Alexander died, the "sword and enemy" he hoped would remain far away descended on them. Alexander's kingdom was divided up. Eventually Antiochus III, the king of Syria, conquered Judea. Antiochus was a Greek. His

son bore the same name and was also Greek.

The son, Antiochus IV, tried to take away the religious freedom of the Jews. He wanted the Jews to act like Greeks and to worship Zeus, the main Greek god, and all other Greek gods.

"Greek ideas are best," Antiochus said. "Speak Greek. Act like Greeks. Pray to Greek gods." He promised riches to Jews who would adopt Greek ways.

Some Jews did. But most did not. The leader of the Jews was Mattathias Hasmon, a priest from Modin, a city not far from Jerusalem. He said, "There is but one God who is God in heaven above and on earth below."

Antiochus mocked the idea of the Jewish God. "One God?" he said. "We have many, all with names. Not invisible and faceless, like your God!"

The Jews refused to turn away from their God. And Antiochus hated them for that. "I will make Jerusalem a cemetery for Jews," he cried in anger.

He issued a decree which said:

> Antiochus, king of Judea and commander of the army, to the Jews. Be warned. Anyone caught praying to God or obeying the Jewish law will be killed. ALL JEWS MUST BECOME GREEK AND BOW DOWN TO ZEUS.

The Jews were frightened. But they would

not change. Nothing could make them worship Zeus. Their ancestors had promised God to worship Him and Him alone. It was a covenant, a treaty. And they would keep the covenant even at the cost of their lives.

They continued to study their holy books in secret, and secretly they kept the Jewish law. But one day two women were caught when Antiochus' soldiers came upon them circumcising their infant sons. The soldiers seized the infants and killed them, then forced the women to parade around the city with the babies around their necks. At the end of the day, when everyone in Jerusalem had seen the spectacle,

the soldiers threw the mothers from a rooftop and killed them.

Antiochus thought surely the Jews would now be so frightened that they would give in. He knew they gathered at their Temple on Friday evenings and Saturday mornings, so he placed a statue of Zeus on the altar which stood outside the Temple. On Friday evening, as the Jews began to arrive at the Temple, he rode his chariot into the Temple square.

"You have seen what happens to those who disobey my decree," Antiochus said. "Now will you bow down to Zeus?"

Mattathias, the priest from Modin, had come to Jerusalem for the Sabbath with his wife and five sons, Judah, Jonathan, Simeon, Eleazar, and Yochanan.

"We do not bow down to idols," Mattathias answered.

Antiochus rode away in anger. In the morning he took his revenge. His soldiers stormed the Temple, killing countless Jews. Then they burned the furniture and holy books and stole the golden lampstand and other precious objects in the Temple.

Oil for the lampstand was kept in small containers called cruses. The soldiers emptied all the cruses over the floor, making it thick with oil, then smeared filth on the walls. As a final insult, they sent pigs into the Temple to dirty it.

THE JEWS
FIGHT BACK

The Jews were heartsick. Their Temple had been defiled so that they could no longer worship there. They sprinkled ashes on their heads to show they were in mourning.

Satisfied, Antiochus put his generals in charge of Judea and left for Egypt to fight a war. Before he departed, he instructed one of his officers to try to bribe Mattathias. "If the Jews see the high priest bow down to Zeus, they will all do the same," he said.

The officer went to Modin and set up an altar in the town square. He put a statue of Zeus at the top of some stones and burned a pig below in sacrifice. Then he sent his soldiers from house to house to round up the Jews.

When Mattathias arrived with his family, the officer held up a bag of gold. He whispered in the priest's ear: "The king offers you this gold if you will bow down to Zeus. He doesn't care if you mean it; just bow down, so your followers will do the same."

"We bow down only to God!" Mattathias answered.

A Jew standing next to him overheard and feared for his life. "I will bow down," the man said, and ran to the altar. Filled with contempt for the disloyal Jew, Mattathias seized the officer's sword and killed the man, then turned on the stunned officer and killed him, too.

"Let us flee, Father," Mattathias' sons called, "before the soldiers return."

Mattathias faced the crowd. "Antiochus will not rest until he has destroyed us," he said. "We must fight back. It is better to die for God than to live as slaves. Whoever is ready to fight for God, come with me."

The priest, his wife, their sons and daughters-in-law and grandchildren went to live in caves, in the hills. They took their livestock with them. Other families came. The Jews of Modin knew the hills of Judea well. Antiochus' soldiers would never be able to find them.

Each day more and more Jewish families arrived. They slept beneath the stars in fair weather and inside the caves in the rainy season. As they had done on the plains, they sent their sheep to graze on the hillsides and planted wheat and barley.

When the community was settled, Mattathias rose up to speak to them. "Everyone must learn to fight," he said. "My son Judah

has been a mighty warrior from his youth. He will lead you. Though our law says we must rest on the Sabbath, if it is a matter of life and death, we will fight back. God needs live servants, not dead law-keepers.''

Thus, in 168 B.C.E. pious Jews became warriors. B.C.E. stands for "Before the Common Era." Jews divide historic times differently from Christians. To Jews, the Christian Era is the Common Era. B.C.E. is the Jewish abbreviation for the same period of time as B.C., which means "Before Christ."

Judah began to train the men and women in the hills. In the daytime he taught them to move about stealthily and to use bows and arrows, slingshots and stones, and daggers.

Each night, under cover of darkness, he sent people down from the hills. They slipped into the nearby towns and villages, past the noses of guards. There they gathered food and weapons from the Jews who had remained behind, and they slew dozens of soldiers at a time.

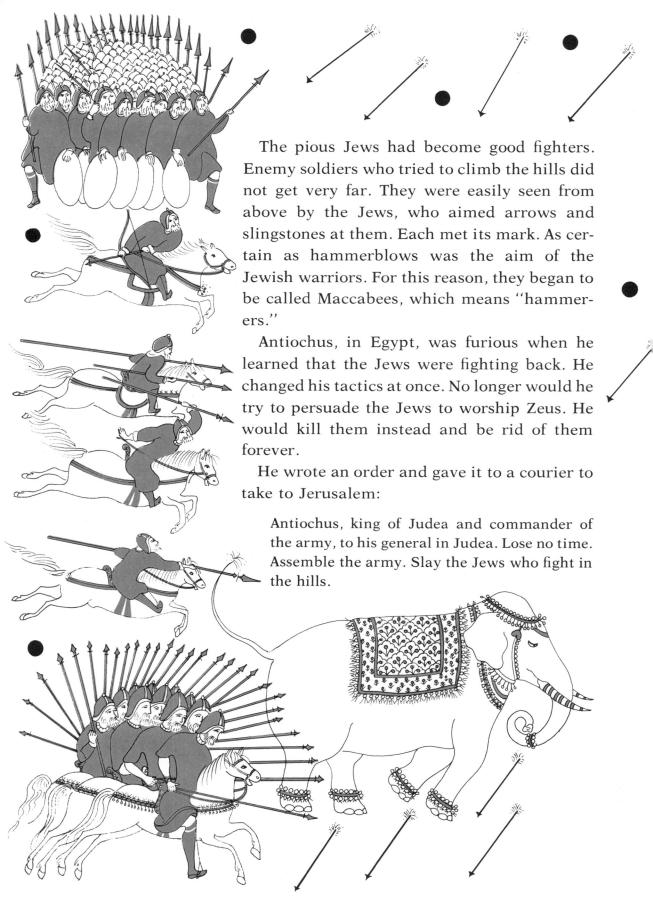

The pious Jews had become good fighters. Enemy soldiers who tried to climb the hills did not get very far. They were easily seen from above by the Jews, who aimed arrows and slingstones at them. Each met its mark. As certain as hammerblows was the aim of the Jewish warriors. For this reason, they began to be called Maccabees, which means "hammerers."

Antiochus, in Egypt, was furious when he learned that the Jews were fighting back. He changed his tactics at once. No longer would he try to persuade the Jews to worship Zeus. He would kill them instead and be rid of them forever.

He wrote an order and gave it to a courier to take to Jerusalem:

> Antiochus, king of Judea and commander of the army, to his general in Judea. Lose no time. Assemble the army. Slay the Jews who fight in the hills.

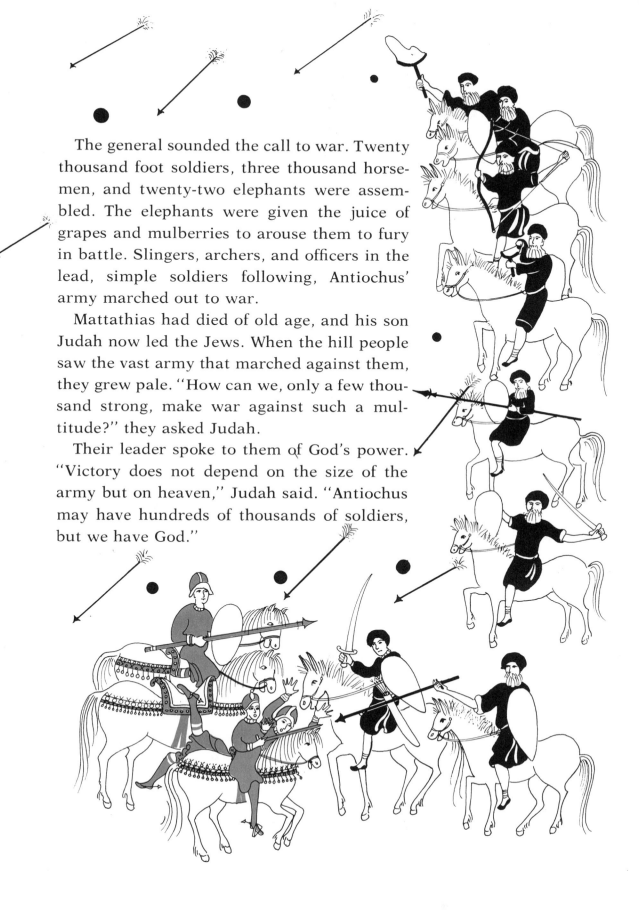

The general sounded the call to war. Twenty thousand foot soldiers, three thousand horsemen, and twenty-two elephants were assembled. The elephants were given the juice of grapes and mulberries to arouse them to fury in battle. Slingers, archers, and officers in the lead, simple soldiers following, Antiochus' army marched out to war.

Mattathias had died of old age, and his son Judah now led the Jews. When the hill people saw the vast army that marched against them, they grew pale. "How can we, only a few thousand strong, make war against such a multitude?" they asked Judah.

Their leader spoke to them of God's power. "Victory does not depend on the size of the army but on heaven," Judah said. "Antiochus may have hundreds of thousands of soldiers, but we have God."

Encouraged by his words, the Jewish people took up their weapons. Until then they had largely defended themselves in small-scale guerrilla battles. Now war began in earnest.

Day and night, Jewish arrows and stones rained down on Antiochus' soldiers. Jewish spies went among the enemy and learned their secrets. When the enemy soldiers tried to mount an attack, the Maccabees lay in wait between the hills and foiled it. Judah sent Maccabees into the enemy camp, catching soldiers off guard and killing many. In a daring raid the Maccabees succeeded in killing the lead elephant. With their leader gone, the other elephants panicked and trampled hundreds of Antiochus' soldiers to death.

The Jews were made strong by their faith in God.

One day Judah's spies returned with a report that the enemy was planning a raid. A detachment of soldiers was on the way to the hills to kill the Jews in a surprise attack. Judah made plans for a counterattack.

Judah lit torches in the hills, as if he and his men were present. Then he and his warriors went down the other side of the hills and arrived in the enemy camp from another direction. They surprised the soldiers guarding the camp and slew them. The Maccabees remained at the camp, waiting for the detachment to return from the hills. When the enemy soldiers came back, they were worn out from searching for the missing Jews. The Maccabees fell upon the tired and befuddled soldiers and slew them.

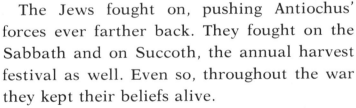

The Jews fought on, pushing Antiochus' forces ever farther back. They fought on the Sabbath and on Succoth, the annual harvest festival as well. Even so, throughout the war they kept their beliefs alive.

Eleazar, Judah's brother, read to them at night under the stars from the Torah, the Book of the Law. For the children, he had stories. He told them about their ancestors: Abraham and Sarah; Isaac and Rebekah; Jacob and both his wives, Leah and Rachel. He also told them about Moses, who had received the Law on Mount Sinai.

After three years of fighting, the enemy soldiers saw that they could not defeat the Jews. They lost heart, and the will to fight left them. Giving up, they put down their weapons and went home.

When Antiochus learned that his men had been defeated by the Jews, he was so ashamed that he drowned himself in the sea.

No one was sorry.

25

The Jews, free at last, came down from the hills. As a first step, they reclaimed and reconquered Jerusalem. When they saw the Temple, they wept. It was covered with filth, animals roamed around inside, and grasses grew on the floor as high as the windows.

"Come, let us clean the Temple and make it pure again," Judah said. "Then we will rededicate it to God."

The people took up buckets and brushes and began to clean the Temple. They made new furniture and a new lampstand. The holy men made new sacred books.

"Look," a woman called as she swept. She held up a cruse of oil from the old days that she had found.

Everyone gathered around her to see it.

Judah examined the cruse. "It is enough to burn for only one day," he said. "But look . . . The seal of the priest is still on it, and the oil is holy."

The people rejoiced over the oil.

When the work was over, the Temple was once more sacred and ready for use. The seven-branch lampstand, the menorah, stood again in the Temple courtyard. The menorah was an eternal light, meant to burn at all times. Its seven cups were filled with the holy oil. Now it could be lit again—only for one day, until new holy oil could be made.

On the twenty-fifth day of the Jewish month of Kislev, in the year 165 B.C.E., Jews arrived in Jerusalem from all over the land. Private homes were crowded with guests. Inns over-flowed. In the evening everyone went to the Temple courtyard to see the lights of the menorah being lit and to hear Judah and the priests rededicate the Temple to God.

The Jews had not known such joy for years. They sang and danced in the streets as they thanked God for delivering them from the hands of their enemies. For three years the Jews had been deprived of the use of their Temple. And for three years they had not celebrated Succoth, the annual harvest festival. They made up for lost time. Each day for eight days they thanked God for the riches that the earth puts forth. Holding branches of palm, myrtle, and willow in one hand and an etrog, a citrus fruit, in the other, they paraded around inside the Temple, chanting praises to God, the Creator of all that is.

On the eighth day they found a source of yet more joy. The oil in the menorah that had been enough to burn for only one day had burned for eight! The people took this as a sign from God. They wept to see it, Judah among them. "Let these events be celebrated with mirth and gladness for all time to come," he said.

With these words, spoken at the dedication of the Temple in Jerusalem some two thousand years ago, the holiday of Hanukkah was born. The word *hanukkah* means "dedication."

HOW THE
HOLIDAY GREW

Judah had decreed that the events be celebrated with "mirth and gladness." But he did
not say what form the celebration should take.
The date, the twenty-fifth of Kislev, was clear.
But what should people do to celebrate? And
how long should the holiday last?

Among the Jews, such matters are decided
by the sages of each age. So these and related
questions were left to the learned rabbis to
answer.

The rabbis of Judah's time declared that
three events were to be celebrated: the recap-
ture of Jerusalem by the heroic Maccabees, the
rededication of the Temple, and the miracle of
the oil.

The life-style of the time shaped the celebration. Oil was the only source of light then. It
was burned in a menorah, a seven-branch
lampstand. Each of the seven cups was filled
with oil, a wick was floated in each cup, and
the menorah was lit.

Many a Jewish home had a seven-branch
lampstand of one design or another. It was a

reminder of the great menorah that stood in the Temple courtyard, and a symbol of the Jewish faith.

The rabbis decreed that the holiday should be celebrated by the burning of lights, in imitation of the lights that were lit in the Temple courtyard when Judah and the Maccabees rededicated the Temple to God. Olive oil was recommended as the preferred oil, since it was the purest oil and also the one that had been found in the Temple cruse.

But olive oil was expensive. And the rabbis wanted everyone to be able to celebrate. So they said any oil was acceptable, just so long as lamps were lit.

In the years that followed, people dutifully burned lights on the twenty-fifth of Kislev. But there was no form to it. Some burned one light; some, two; others burned a light for each member of the family. Some burned lights for one night; some, for all eight. Clearly something was missing; the celebration was unformed. A holiday feeling was absent from the home. The lights gave off no special glow. It was understandable. The lights that were lit for the holiday were the same ones that were lit every day.

The rabbis had to do something to make the celebration more felt and more special. They

debated the matter and finally came to some
decisions. To give the holiday more form, the
rabbis declared that it was to be celebrated for
eight days, from the day of the rededication, on
the twenty-fifth, to the last day that the oil
burned. They also asked that the design of the
lampstand be changed. It would now have
eight branches, one for each day, and would be
used only for the holiday and at no other time.
Thus, the eight-branch lampstand entered the
holiday and soon became its symbol.

Some four or five hundred years after the Maccabees, candles were invented. Many people still clung to the oil that their ancestors had used, and even today Jews all over the world continue to burn oil to celebrate the holiday. But candles, as a new and easy source of light, became the most common means of illumination, and some Jews began using them in their menorahs.

Then another problem arose. The lights that were kindled on the holiday were lit for the glory of God and were meant only to shine. Yet people began to make use of their holiday candles to work by or to use the flame from a holi-
y candle to kindle other candles.

 means had to be found to preserve the sa-
 nature of the lights. The rabbis studied the
ter, then called for yet another refinement
e menorah. Instead of eight cups, they
 for a lampstand with nine cups. The
cup was to be placed on a different plane
he others, either a little higher or a little
This was to set it apart, so it would not
used with the sacred lights.

andle in the ninth cup was called a
h in Hebrew and *shammes* in Yiddish.
ls mean the same thing, "servant" or
 As the name implies, the *shammes*
o do. It is kindled first, and its flame

and only its flame is used to kindle the other eight candles. Once the *shammes* came into use, the sacred nature of the other eight candles could be preserved. They could flicker away undisturbed and just glow.

The placement of the lampstand was subject to change. In Judea, where Jews lived in their own land, it hung outside the home, to announce the holiday. The practice endured until Roman legions overran Judea and occupied it. The Romans were idol worshipers who did not approve of the Jewish faith. Nor did the Jews wish to provoke their new rulers. To remove an area of possible complaint, the rabbis decreed that the menorah be taken inside the house and kept in the window.

There were times, because of the harshness of Roman rule, when the Jews could not celebrate Hanukkah or any other expression of their faith. Many Jews fled to other lands in search of religious freedom. They found a haven in Spain and were once more free enough to display lights in the windows of their homes during Hanukkah. After several centuries of peace the Jews again found themselves in trouble. As Antiochus had done in the days of the Maccabees, the Spanish rulers demanded that the Jews give up their religious beliefs. In 1492 Queen Isabella and King Fer-

dinand expelled 200,000 Jews from Spain.

The Spanish Jews fled to a number of other lands. Meanwhile, many other Jews from Germany settled in Poland. When Poland came under Russian rule, Jews were restricted to certain sections of the city. They were permitted to live and work only in those sections.

Periodically Russian and Polish soldiers attacked the Jews, often during Hanukkah or some other holiday, and usually violently. The attacks were known as pogroms, and the government permitted them to take place. Jews realized it was dangerous to call attention to themselves during a holiday. The rabbis ruled that in times of trouble the Hanukkah lampstand could be kept inside, away from the window and public view.

Today Jews live as free citizens in many countries of the world. And the nine-branch lampstand can often be seen lighting up the windows of Jewish homes during Hanukkah.

The Hanukkah lampstand has now received a name of its own. The seven-branch lampstand is still called a menorah, as it was in the days of the Maccabees, when it stood in the Temple courtyard. The menorah is the symbol of the state of Israel. One version of it or another can be found in many Jewish homes, where it is used as a decoration and also as a source of light. To distinguish the nine-cup lampstand from the traditional menorah, the Hanukkah lampstand is today called a *hanukkiah.*

Even the name of the holiday has undergone changes. Lights, or Festival of Lights, is what it was called in the olden days. The name *Hanukkah* was not in general use. But the rabbis saw an undesirable trend developing. More and more, people were paying honor to the military victories of the Maccabees. The religious meanings of the holiday were dwindling in importance, and the rededication of the Temple was mentioned only casually. This worried the rabbis. They felt that if such a trend were permitted to continue, the religious aspects of the holiday might disappear altogether from the celebration.

To prevent this from happening, the rabbis changed the name of the holiday from Lights to Hanukkah. Since the word means "dedication," it awakens memories of the Maccabees and the rededication of the Temple. With the name change, the rabbis won a permanent place for the religious aspects of the holiday in its celebration.

THE JEWISH CALENDAR

Hanukkah starts on the twenty-fifth day of the Jewish month of Kislev. Just when does that fall in the Christian year? To determine this, it is necessary to look at the Gregorian calendar, which is in use throughout the world.

The Gregorian calendar was introduced by Pope Gregory XIII in the sixteenth century. It has 365 days and 12 months, January through December.

The Jewish calendar has 354 days. It, too, has 12 months: Tishri, Heshvan, Kislev, Tevet, Shevat, Adar, Nisan, Iyar, Sivan, Tammuz, Av, Elul.

But there are many differences between the two calendars.

The Gregorian calendar begins with the birth of Jesus, almost two thousand years ago. Time is reckoned from the time of Jesus, who is called Christ (means "messiah" in Greek) by Christians. The time period B.C. means "Before Christ." The period after the birth of Jesus is A.D. This stands for the Latin term *anno domini,* "in the year of [our] Lord." The Maccabees lived some 165 years before Jesus was born.

Recorded Jewish time is reckoned quite differently. It begins with the story of Creation, which the ancient rabbis placed at the year 3760 before Jesus was born. That, added to the Gregorian year, turns up the date of the Jewish year—e.g., 3760 plus 1982 is the Jewish year 5742. Jews call the period after Jesus' birth the Common Era (c.e.). Judah then lived Before the Common Era (b.c.e.).

The Jewish year has more than one beginning. The main beginning is in the fall, when the calendar opens with the month of Tishri. The Jewish new year is celebrated in that month. It signifies a year in the religious life of the Jew, the year of the individual in his or her relationship with God.

There is another beginning, in the spring. More than three thousand years ago the Jews were slaves in Egypt. Moses freed them and wandered with them toward the Promised Land. Just as Israel was known as Judea in the days of the Maccabees, it was called Canaan in Moses's times. To the Jews it was the Promised Land. The wandering Jews entered Canaan in the month of Nisan, an event that changed Jewish history. Now the Jews ceased being slaves and wanderers and became a nation. Nisan marks the first month in the existence of the Jewish nation.

There is also a new year for trees. It falls on the fifteenth day of the month of Shevat (January). Israel, a Mediterranean country, has two main seasons: a long, dry summer and a few months of winter rains. In Shevat winter is almost over and almond trees are in blossom. And on the fifteenth day of the month, farmers and schoolchildren plant new trees and pray for weather that will allow the trees to grow to maturity.

In the Jewish week, Sunday is the first day and Saturday the last. Saturday, as the seventh day, is the Jewish Sabbath. Jewish days do not have names. They are referred to by their position in the week: first day, second day, and so on, through the sixth day. Only Saturday, the Sabbath, has a name—*Shabbat* in Hebrew, *Shabbos* in Yiddish. The Maccabees fought for the right to keep the Jewish Sabbath.

The duration of the Jewish day, too, is different. Jewish law demanded that certain rituals be performed on holidays and on the Sabbath. People needed to know exactly when the day began and when it ended. The ancient rabbis studied the skies for an answer to this question: Just when does a day begin? They concluded that a day starts when the sun goes down and that it ends twenty-four hours later, when it is dark enough to see three stars.

Thus, the Jewish day starts not at midnight, but at sunset. A day begins the evening before. Hanukkah commences, therefore, not on the twenty-fifth of Kislev, but the evening before, on the twenty-fourth.

A Jewish calendar, which carries the days of the Christian year alongside those of the Jewish year, shows on just what day in December the twenty-fifth of Kislev falls.

THE TEMPLE

The Temple at which the Jews worshiped, and which the Maccabees rededicated in 165 B.C.E., was erected some eight hundred years before. It was built by King Solomon in 955 B.C.E. to hold the Law that Moses received on Mount Sinai, and it was the first permanent Jewish shrine.

Solomon's reign was one of peace and splendor. His father, King David, only dreamed of building a temple to God. But Solomon made the dream come true. He hired the best architects and artisans to build the temple. But he lacked timber. There was no timber in Judea. There were, however, great quantities of it in the north, in the forests of Lebanon.

Solomon wrote to his friend Hiram, king of Tyre, the ancient capital of Lebanon and the most powerful city on the Mediterranean. The two rulers concluded a trade agreement. Hiram promised to supply Solomon with labor and logs in exchange for surplus olive oil and wheat from Judea. Hiram's men felled cedar and firs for Solomon in the forests of Lebanon and floated them down to him on the sea to the ancient port of Joppa, called Jaffa today.

Solomon built the Temple on Mount Moriah in Jerusalem, the city his father had chosen as his capital. He built it according to the measurements set out in the First Book of Kings in the Bible. The Temple proper took seven years to complete. Its inside walls were ornamented with carved wooden figures of angels, trees, and flowers, all overlaid with gold. Inside and out, it was a marvel of design.

Distinguished visitors came from far and wide to attend the dedication ceremony and feast, which together lasted seven days. Solomon entertained his guests royally. For their eating pleasure, he slaughtered 22,000 oxen and 120,000 sheep and he fattened countless fowl. The music of harps and lutes filled the air.

At the dedication in the courtyard before the Temple Solomon blessed the guests. Then he fell on his knees and spoke to God, saying, "I have built thee a lofty Temple to dwell in, a settled place for thee to abide in forever."

But the Temple was not to be the settled place for the spirit of God to dwell in forever, as Solomon had hoped. It was destroyed and rebuilt again and again.

Some 350 years later, King Nebuchadnezzar of Babylon captured Jerusalem, in 586 B.C.E. On the ninth day of the Jewish month of Av (July–August), he destroyed the Temple. As spoils of war, Nebuchadnezzar took the golden lampstand and other Temple treasures. He exiled all the priests, scholars, and other educated Jews to Babylon and allowed only the vinedressers and other peasant laborers to remain in Jerusalem.

In a later war Nebuchadnezzar was himself defeated by Cyrus of Persia. Cyrus was a creative ruler. He believed that cities grew great when they had mixed populations, with each group contributing its own special skills and talents. He returned to the Jews the treasures Nebuchadnezzar had taken from them and urged them to go back to Jerusalem and rebuild the Temple.

Many Jews remained in Babylon. More than forty-two thousand returned to Jerusalem. The Temple on Mount Moriah was rebuilt in 519 B.C.E. The Second Temple, as it is known, was simple, unadorned, and much more humble than Solomon's. Except for the three years of the Maccabean war, it continued in use for the next six hundred years. It was in the courtyard of this Second Temple that the holiday of Hanukkah was born.

In 63 B.C.E. Rome ruled the Western world. Romans worshiped their pagan gods. Bringing their beliefs and customs with them, Roman soldiers marched into Jerusalem and occupied

47

it. This brought Jewish rule to an end. Oppressed by the Romans, many Jews fled. Those who remained looked after the Temple. It was the center of their lives.

Herod, a wealthy Jewish prince from Idumea, south of Judea, had many important friends in Rome, Marc Antony among them. Some sources say that Herod was half Jewish; some, that his family had been converts to Judaism after the Maccabean war. Whatever the case, he was not a committed Jew. He preferred the customs and life-style of the Romans.

Because of his connections in Rome, Herod succeeded in getting himself appointed king of the Jews. His great wealth had allowed him to become a great builder. Earlier he had built palaces for himself and such public buildings as stadia and baths for the citizenry. Now, to impress Rome and also to win favor with the Jews, Herod rebuilt the Temple.

The sanctuary remained the same, but Herod added platforms and porches and porticoes, greatly enlarging the Temple complex. Herod's Temple was much more lavish and beautiful even than Solomon's. Some considered it the most beautiful building in the world. While actually a third Temple, because of the extensive additions, it is still called the Second Temple.

When Herod died, Rome took a firmer hold on Judea. Soon the land was no longer known by that name. It was changed to Palestine.

Unwilling to submit to the foreign conquerors, the Jews revolted and fought back. For a time it looked as if their revolt might be successful. But the might of Rome was too great. With fire and battering rams, Roman soldiers destroyed the Temple and laid waste to

Jerusalem. In 70 C.E., after a thousand years of existence, the Temple disappeared altogether from Jewish life.

The Jews who had defended the Temple were captured and thrown to wild animals in the arenas. Others were taken to Rome, where they were paraded around the city in chains or sold into slavery.

The day that the Second Temple was destroyed was the ninth of Av, the same day on which Nebuchadnezzar had destroyed the first Temple more than six hundred years before. The ninth of Av is a day of fasting and mourning for Orthodox Jews.

Today the splendor and greatness of the Temple are gone, but a section of the wall that surrounded it remains. This was formerly called the Wailing Wall because of the many Jews who came there to weep over the destruction of the Temple and the loss of Jerusalem. Today it is called *Ha-kotel Ha-Ma'aravi*, the Western Wall. Jews go there to pray on the Sabbath, Hanukkah, all holidays, and every day. They stand close to it or lean against it. The sky is overhead. It is a holy place. With the large numbers of people coming there daily to pray or meditate, it has become a structure at which to worship, a temple without walls.

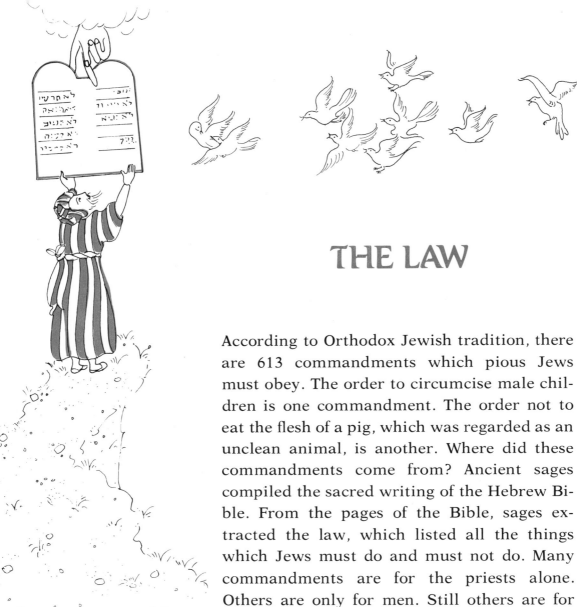

THE LAW

According to Orthodox Jewish tradition, there are 613 commandments which pious Jews must obey. The order to circumcise male children is one commandment. The order not to eat the flesh of a pig, which was regarded as an unclean animal, is another. Where did these commandments come from? Ancient sages compiled the sacred writing of the Hebrew Bible. From the pages of the Bible, sages extracted the law, which listed all the things which Jews must do and must not do. Many commandments are for the priests alone. Others are only for men. Still others are for women, or farmers, or other groups of people. The Maccabees, who were pious Jews, obeyed the commandments that applied to them.

These are the Ten Commandments that Moses received from God on Mount Sinai:

I am the Lord your God who brought you out of
    Egypt, out of the house of bondage.
You shall have no other gods before me.
You shall not use my name in vain.
You shall keep the Sabbath holy, to honor Cre-
    ation.
You shall honor your father and mother.
You shall not murder.
You shall not commit adultery.
You shall not steal.
You shall not falsely accuse nor swear to an
    untruth.
You shall not envy your neighbor.

When Moses came down from Mount Sinai
with the commandments, he read them aloud.
The people heard and accepted them, saying,
"Whatever God commands we will do and we
will obey."

This promise on the part of the Jews of
Moses' time to keep the law is a treaty, or covenant, that they made with God. More than a
thousand years later the Jews of the Maccabean period fought to keep it.

HOW THE HOLIDAY IS CELEBRATED

All over the world, when Hanukkah comes around, candles are lit at sunset in Jewish homes. The person who has been chosen to kindle the lights strikes a match, lights the *shammes*, and with its flame lights the other candles. On the first night, one candle is lit, on the second, two, until on the eighth night all nine are burning brightly. Candles are inserted in the lampstand from right to left, the direction in which the Hebrew language is written. They are lit from left to right, the newest candle first.

On the first night, three blessings are said:

[Before the candles are kindled] Blessed art thou, O Lord, our God, King of the universe, who has sanctified us with thy commandments and bidden us to kindle the Hanukkah lights.

[During the kindling] Blessed art thou, O Lord, our God, King of the universe, who did wondrous things for our ancestors in times past in this very season. We kindle these lights in honor of thy holy miracles. The lights are sacred. We do not make use of them but only look upon them in order to give thanks to thy great name.

[Also during the kindling] Blessed art thou, O Lord, our God, King of the universe, who has kept us alive and well and allowed us to reach this season.

On the other seven nights, the third blessing is eliminated and only the first two are said.

The holiday songs are "Mi Yimalel" ("Speaking of Wonders"), "Hanukkah Oi Hanukkah," and "Maoz Tzur" ("Rock of Ages"). The most popular is "Rock of Ages," sung after the lights have been kindled. It was written in the thirteenth century by a Jewish poet known only as Mordechai. The words of the first stanza are:

Ma-oz Tzur	Rock of ages,
ye-shu a-ti	you are all,
le-ka na-eh le-sha-bei-ak.	there is none supremer.
Ti-kon beit te-fi-la-ti	Fortress, cliff and citadel,
ve-sham to-da ne-za bei-ak.	savior and redeemer.
Le-eit ta-kin mat-bei-ak,	Enemies assailed us,
mi-tzar ha-me-na-bei-ak,	but thy might availed us,
az eg-mor be-shir miz-mor,	thy great spark lit the dark
Ha-nu-kat ha-miz-bei-ak.	when our own strength failed us.

Instead of singing this song, Jews of Spanish origin follow another custom when the lights have been lit. They recite the Thirtieth Psalm. The opening words are:

> We will praise you, O Lord, for you have lifted us up and have not allowed our enemies to rejoice over us.

It is easy to see why the holiday is a favorite of children. Each evening, as candles are lit, a festive air fills the home. Voices raised in song heighten the mood of celebration. While adults have their own pastimes, children like to while away the evening playing dreidel before the flickering candles. Dreidel is the name of both the toy that the game is played with, a small spinning top, and the game itself. So closely is the dreidel identified with Hanukkah that it is often used as a symbol for the holiday.

A dreidel may be made of wood, plastic, or metal and has four sides. Four Hebrew letters are inscribed on it, one letter on each side.

ג —*gimmel (G)*   נ —*nun (N)*

שׁ —*shin (SH)*   ה —*heh (H)*

The letters stand for the Hebrew words *Nes Gadol Hayah Sham*, which means "A Great

Miracle Happened There."

A spinning top is an ancient toy. Legend tells us that it played a part in those days so long ago when Antiochus forbade the study of Hebrew books. According to some stories, if the children were studying the forbidden books and saw Antiochus' soldiers approaching, they hid the books and quickly took out a dreidel, as if they had been playing all along.

In those days the dreidel had no letters on it. The letters were added in the thirteenth century in Germany, where the game as it is played today originated. To play, children gather around a table or, more commonly, sit on the floor. They make a pot of whatever is available in quantity—nuts, raisins, marbles, toothpicks, pennies, or the like. Someone takes up the dreidel and spins it, and the children take turns spinning.

If the letter *nun* (*N*) is turned up, the player gets nothing. If *gimmel* (*G*) is turned up, this is *Gadol,* or great, and the player wins the whole pot. If *heh* (*H*), the player wins half the pot. *Shin* (*SH*) stands for *shlemiel.* This is a Yiddish word for a person with two left feet or what is known as a real loser. The player turning up this letter drops out of the game or else contributes to the pot to stay in.

There are many variations to the game. Sometimes a number is assigned to a letter and the game is played for points. The person with the most points wins. Sometimes a history game is played. The letter that is turned up must relate to an event that the Maccabees lived through.

For example, a player who gets the letter *nun* (*N*) might call out, "Not allowed." The *gimmel* (*G*) might stand for, say, "Greek is good for Greeks." *Heh* (*H*) could stand for "Hebrew is good for Hebrews" or "Hebrews 10, Antiochus 0." A possibility for *shin* (*SH*) is *Shabbos,* which means "Sabbath."

Whatever the game, it is played only for small stakes and only for fun because gambling is a forbidden activity.

In Israel the dreidel toy is slightly altered. One of the four letters is different, and for good reason. The letter *shin* (*SH*) stands for the word *sham*, which means "there." But Israel, or Judea, is where the revolt of the Maccabees took place. In Israel the letter *shin* has been replaced with the letter *peh* (P). It stands for the word *po*, which means "here."

The entire phrase in Israel, *Nes Gadol Hayah Po*, has a double meaning. It recalls the victory of the Maccabees in 165 B.C.E., but it also recalls a very great, and quite similar, event which took place in our own times. In 1948 the land of Israel was known as Palestine. That year the Jews once more fought a war of independence, this time with the armies of several nations. Like the Maccabees, the modern Jews reclaimed Jerusalem and won back their ancient homeland, which had been under foreign control for almost two thousand years. The Jewish nation was reborn, and the modern state of Israel was created.

In Israel, where Hanukkah is often called the Feast of Lights, the holiday is a nonstop festival. Schools are closed, and businesses shut down. A mood of celebration takes over as people rush to parties, picnics, and sporting events or travel to the villages and cities they have been planning to visit for weeks. For eight nights, lights blaze in the windows of every home and from huge electric lamplights atop public buildings.

Old customs are still followed, too. In the safety of their own land many Jews still cling to the ways of their ancestors. Batei Warsawer (Houses of Warsaw) is an old Jewish section in the city of Jerusalem. It was built about a hundred years ago by and for Jews from Warsaw, Poland. On Hanukkah this neighborhood of old stone houses and cobblestone courtyards has the appearance of a timeless Jewish city. Outside every home hangs a glass-enclosed hanukkiah that burns oil for eight nights. The direct ancestors of these people did the same in the ghettos of Europe, and their ancestors began the practice in Judea long centuries ago.

The main event of the holiday is provided by Israel's famous sports club, the Maccabees, named for Judah and his fighters. The runners, the chief players, welcome the holiday with a relay race.

In Modin, the town where Mattathias lived and where Judah and his brothers are buried, a large bonfire is built. The runner who has been chosen to start the race dips his torch into the flames and runs with it to the next town, where he hands it over to the runner who will take it on from there. The last stop is Jerusalem. Thousands of people line the roads between Modin and Jerusalem, waiting to see the Torch of Freedom, as it is known, go by.

In Jerusalem the runner comes to a halt at the Western Wall. There he hands over the torch to the chief rabbi, who uses it to kindle the first light in a giant oil-burning hanukkiah that is enclosed in glass. On hand for the ceremony are the president of the country and the thousands of people who have come to watch the lights being kindled.

FOODS

Most Jewish holiday customs, whether they are things to do or foods to eat, have come about in such a way that everyone may participate in the celebration. The traditional foods of

Hanukkah are an example. The ingredients are readily available and cheap enough to be within reach of even the poorest person.

Among Jews whose ancestors lived in communities where German, Polish, Russian, or another European language was spoken, the typical Hanukkah dish is *latkes*. These are potato pancakes fried in oil. The oil is used as a reminder of the miracle of the burning oil.

Jews of Spanish origin celebrate with vegetable pancakes, or *bourmuelos*, a crispy ball of fried dough that has been dipped in honey.

The Jews of Israel and those who come from the other lands of the Middle East, such as Syria, Iraq, Iran, celebrate with a similar pastry—*soofganiyot*. These are a form of jelly doughnut covered with powdered sugar.

There is a curious legend about *soofganiyot*. It goes back much farther than the days of the Maccabees, to the time of Adam and Eve. According to the story, when the Almighty drove Adam and Eve from the Garden of Eden, He gave them a sweet pastry to comfort them, as a sort of consolation prize. The singular of *soofganiyot* is *soofganiya*, or, broken down into three words, *sof gan yh*, which in Hebrew means "end of the Garden of God." Can it be that Adam and Eve were munching on *soofganiyot* as they left the Garden of Eden?

HANUKKAH GELT

Hanukkah gelt in Yiddish means "Hanukkah money." According to some sources, the giving of coins at Hanukkah time originated in the seventeenth century in Poland. It was the custom at Hanukkah for parents to hand their children money to distribute among their teachers. The teachers were poorly paid, and the extra money from parents provided them with a bonus.

In time, as Jews became more affluent, children were given *Hanukkah gelt* to keep for themselves. The custom took hold and eventually spread around the world. In most communities only children are given *Hanukkah gelt*. The amounts are always small, usually just a few coins, and as a rule, the children do not get to keep them all. Many homes have charity boxes for coins. Such boxes may also be found in Hebrew schools and neighborhood stores. Children are encouraged to put some of their *Hanukkah gelt* in the boxes for donation to various charities.

According to other sources, coins have a much more important meaning in the Hanukkah celebration. They are symbolic of the ancient rule of the Maccabees. The coins that were in use in Judea when Antiochus ruled

were Greek and portrayed Greek personalities or themes. But when the Maccabees won the war and reclaimed Jerusalem, they won control of the government. As an expression of sovereignty, they began to mint their own coins. These coins portrayed Jewish subjects.

For similar reasons, coins are an important part of the Hanukkah celebration in Israel. Each year the government issues a special commemorative coin on the holiday. In 1980 Israel changed its form of currency to the sheqel. This is an ancient monetary unit. It is often referred to in the Hebrew Bible and was in use in the days of Abraham. For Hanukkah 1980, Israel issued its first one-sheqel coin. On the face of it is a reproduction of a nineteenth century hanukkiah from Corfu, an island off the coast of Greece.

GIFTS

Along with the fun and games, Hanukkah is a time also to give gifts. There is no formula, no set routine. The gifts may be small or large. What is given and when depend on the individual family. Some people give a gift on the first night of the holiday; others, on the last. Some may give gifts on all eight nights. Such gifts are likely to be of the stretched-out sort or tokens—a dreidel one night, a pencil the next, a favorite cookie. Some people may favor the second or fourth or seventh night—or day—for reasons of their own. It is the custom among some families to give each child a hanukkiah and a supply of candles as a present. This allows the child to participate directly in the observance of the holiday and to create yet more light by adding his or her kindled candles to the others.

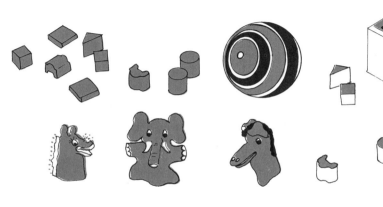

LOCAL CUSTOMS

Jews live and have lived in almost every corner of the world. Since each land has a language and culture of its own, it is not surprising that additional customs have sprung up around the basic Hanukkah celebration.

Long ago, when the Jews fled the Spanish Inquisition in the fifteenth century, many settled in Venice, Italy. The Italian government assigned them the foundry section to live in. "Foundry" in Italian is *getto*, from which the word ghetto derives. This Jewish quarter was the first ghetto. Up to 1797 a great number of Jews lived there. On Hanukkah they would ride up and down the canals of Venice in their gondolas, calling out greetings to relatives and friends.

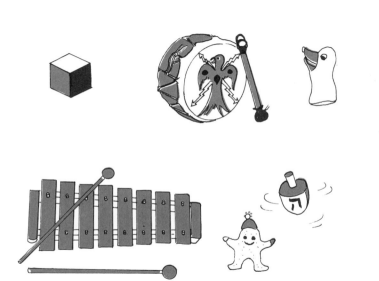

Syrian Jewish children often receive as a gift a candle in the shape of a hand. The hand is a popular symbol of protection in Syria and other lands of the Middle East. People believe it keeps the "evil eye" away. What is the evil eye? It is an unkind thought that exists in the mind, or eye, of an unfriendly person.

Long ago the Jews of Aleppo, Syria, introduced a unique custom at Hanukkah. They used two *shammes* candles. They had fled from the Spanish Inquisition, and after many years of wandering they found a haven in Aleppo. To give thanks, they added the extra *shammes* candle. Today Syria is hostile to the Jews, and very few still live there.

Turkish Jewish children often take a plate of sweet pastries from home and bring them to a

neighbor or relative. Usually they receive a plate of sweets in return.

In some communities of Spanish origin the seventh night of Hanukkah is dedicated to women. They are honored for their bravery during the Maccabean war.

North African Jewish women and girls fill the synagogue at Hanukkah. As a rule, women may not remove the holy scrolls from the ark, where they are kept. This is only for men to do. But on the seventh day of Hanukkah an exception is made. Women may remove the scrolls and kiss them. The rabbi then blesses the women.

Jewish children from Yemen make their own menorahs out of clay. With the coins that they receive, they buy sugar and a red powder which they make into a sweet drink.

Among the Jews of Kurdistan, in northern Iraq and Iran, children carry rough effigies of Antiochus as they go from house to house, asking for *Hanukkah gelt*. At the end of their rounds, they burn the figure and cry, "Antiochus! Antiochus!"

THE UNIVERSAL CUSTOM

Whatever local custom may have been added, the kindling of lights is the basic tradition and the foundation of the holiday celebration. It is performed by all Jews no matter where they live.

So important was the kindling of lights thought to be that Maimonides, the famous Jewish philosopher of the twelfth century, wrote, "Even if a person has no food to eat but what he receives from charity, he should beg, or else sell an item of clothing, in order to have the wherewithal to buy oil and a lamp." Maimonides' words have been heeded. Throughout Jewish history, in good times and bad, the lights of Hanukkah have been kindled.

In bad times Jews have been known to kindle lights even at great personal risk. They did so in the darkest days of Jewish history, in the 1930s and 1940s—when Adolf Hitler set out to conquer the world and annihilate the Jewish nation. This period, which brought about the slaughter of six million Jews, is known as the Holocaust. According to reports of survivors, heart-rending efforts were made by Jews in concentration camps to celebrate Hanukkah. One such episode took place at Bergen-Belsen, a camp near Hanover, Germany.

When Hanukkah arrived, the Nazi guards mocked the Jews who were imprisoned there, asking how they expected to celebrate under the circumstances. One guard handed a package of margarine to the rabbi, saying it was a treat for the Jews. When the rabbi reached out for the margarine, the guard let it drop to the floor and ordered the rabbi to lick it up.

The horrified Jews watched as the rabbi knelt down and licked up the margarine. Then the soldiers left. The Jews thought the rabbi had gone mad when he turned to them with a smile.

While he was on his knees, he had managed to scrape up some of the margarine and hide it on the inside of his jacket. "We have oil," the rabbi said proudly, showing the margarine.

"Also wicks," he added as he pulled threads from the jacket. "Now all we need is a menorah."

The Jews soon had their menorah. One person had a spoon; another, some buttons; another, an empty can. The rabbi placed a drop of margarine and a thread on the odd assortment of eight "cups," then lit the Hanukkah lights. Though feeble, the lights were precious to the Jews in the camp.

Another account comes from Anne Frank, who celebrated Hanukkah in the attic of a house in Amsterdam, Holland, where she and her family hid from the Nazis throughout World War II. In her now-famous diary Anne wrote on the page for December 7, 1942: "We just gave each other a few little presents and then we lit the candles. Because of the shortage of candles, we only had them alight for ten minutes." When the Nazis discovered the attic sometime later, they arrested Anne and her family and carried their hanukkiah away as loot.

Yet another story from the Holocaust concerns Issac Newman, a Jewish teenager in Poland. After they occupied Poland, the Nazis

hunted for Jews to send to concentration camps. A Polish monk saved Isaac by hiding him in the monastery. The monk told no one that the boy was a Jew. As Hanukkah drew near, Isaac felt a need to express his Jewishness. He collected wax from monastery candles and made Hanukkah candles for himself. On the first night, secretly, in a remote corner of the monastery, he lit the candles and said the blessings. As he began to sing softly to himself the words of "Maoz Tzur," he felt a hand on his shoulder. The boy's heart nearly came to a stop. But it was only the kindly monk. "Come, Isaac," the man said. "Let us sing 'Maoz Tzur' together." This they proceeded to do.

Even today there are dangers for Jews in certain countries. The Soviet Union outlaws religion. Jews must obey their religious impulses in secret. A touching story is told by Misha Raitzin, now an American citizen and a singer with the Metropolitan Opera Company. Raitzin lived in Moscow, with Orthodox Jewish parents. They taught him the traditions of his religion in secret. At eighteen, Misha went to Siberia to sing, and when Hanukkah came around, he wanted to do something to celebrate. He whittled a little lampstand out of potatoes in his room. Then, after singing the title role in the opera *Rigoletto,* he locked himself in his room, removed his makeup, put on the skullcap that Orthodox Jewish men wear, and, lighting candles, softly intoned the Hanukkah blessings to himself.

The compulsion to celebrate Hanukkah is strong. In a free society where there is nothing to fear, Jews celebrate it openly with the "mirth and gladness" that Judah called for two thousand years ago. Yet existing side by side with the high spirits of many Jews today is a second set of feelings. Just as the ancient rabbis sought to stress the religious aspects of Hanukkah, the government of Israel today stresses the victories of the Maccabees.

The small land of Israel is surrounded by twenty-two hostile neighbors. The rumblings of war are never far away. Israel bolsters the hearts of its citizens by reminding them that Jews have triumphed before against great odds and that with faith and determination they shall do so again.

Mixing with the mirth and gladness of Hanukkah is a prayerful wish for peace.

GLOSSARY AND PRONUNCIATION GUIDE

Antiochus (an-TI-ok-us) The Syrian-Greek king of Judea

Apocrypha (a-POK-riff-a) A collection of writings of unknown origin which were not included in the Hebrew Bible

Circumcise (SIR-kum-size) To cut off the foreskin of the penis. It is a sign of the covenant, or agreement, between God and the Jewish people

Cruse (krooz) A container for lamp oil

Dreidel (DRAY-dul) A spinning top

Ha-Kotel Ha-Ma' aravi (ha-KO-tel ha-ma-ra-VI) The Western Wall that surrounded the Temple in Jerusalem

Hanukkah (ha-noo-KAH) The Jewish holiday that celebrates the victory of the Maccabees and the rededication of the Temple

Hanukkiah (ha-noo-kee-YA) The nine-branch lampstand for Hanukkah

Judea (ju-DAY-a) The ancient name of Israel

Maccabees (MAC-a-beez) The Jews who fought in the hills

Mattathias (mat-a-THI-us) The priest from Modin who led the revolt against Antiochus

Menorah (men-o-RA) The seven-branch lampstand that is the symbol of the state of Israel

Nes Gadol Hayah Sham (ness ga-DOL ha-ya SHAM) A Great Miracle Happened There

Pagan (PAY-gun) Idol worshiper

Pogrom (po-GRUM) A riot against the Jews

Shabbat (sha-BAHT) The Sabbath, Saturday (Hebrew)

Shabbos (sha-BOS) The Sabbath, Saturday (Yiddish)

Shammash (sha-MAHSH) Servant candle (Hebrew)

Shammes (SHA-miss) Servant candle (Yiddish)

Succoth (sook-OAT) The Jewish fall harvest festival

Synagogue (SIN-a-gog) A Jewish house of worship and assembly

Torah (tow-RAH) The first five books of the Hebrew Bible, also called the law

Zeus (zoose) The chief Greek god

CHRONOLOGY OF THE TEMPLE

The dates are approximate

955 B.C.E.　On Mount Moriah in Jerusalem King Solomon built the first Temple, the center of Jewish life.

586 B.C.E.　Nebuchadnezzar, king of Babylon, captured Jerusalem, destroyed the Temple, and exiled the Jews.

539 B.C.E.　King Cyrus of Persia defeated Nebuchadnezzar and urged Jews to return to Jerusalem and rebuild their temple.

519 B.C.E.　The Jews rebuilt the Temple. This was the Second Temple.

168 B.C.E.　Antiochus IV, Syrian-Greek ruler of Judea, profaned the Temple and forbade Jews to worship God. The Jews took up arms and revolted.

165 B.C.E.　The Jews, led by Judah and the Maccabees, defeated Antiochus' forces and recaptured Jerusalem. They purified and rededicated the Temple.

20 B.C.E.　Herod enlarged and beautified the Second Temple.

70 C.E.　Rome conquered Jerusalem, razed the city, and destroyed the Temple.

77

OTHER BOOKS
ABOUT HANUKKAH

Adler, David A. *Hanukkah Fun Book: Puzzles, Riddles, Magic & More.* New York: Bonim Books, 1976. This is an attractive paperback activity book for ages eight to twelve.

Drucker, Malka. *Hanukkah: Eight Nights, Eight Lights.* New York: Holiday House, 1980. A Hanukkah book for ages eight to eleven, including history, crafts, games, and recipes.

Goodman, Philip. *The Hanukkah Anthology.* Philadelphia: Jewish Publication Society, 1976. Includes stories, customs, plays, poems, activities, and various writings about Hanukkah. For ages eleven and up.

Greenfeld, Howard. *Chanukah.* New York: Holt, Rinehart & Winston, 1976. A dignified retelling of the story of the Maccabees, with emphasis on political and military events. Illustrated by Elaine Grove and handsomely designed by Bea Feitler. For all ages.

Metzger, Bruce M., ed. *The Oxford Annotated Apocrypha*, revised standard edition. New York: Oxford University Press, 1965, 1977. This source book contains all the Books of the Maccabees I, II, III, and IV and Psalm 151, with commentaries.

Singer, Isaac B. *The Power of Light.* New York: Farrar, Straus & Giroux, 1980. A collection of stories about Hanukkah, told by a world-famous storyteller. May be read aloud for group enjoyment and for private pleasure.